Welcome

NAOMI STARKEY

Millions watched the swearing-in of the new US President Barack Obama in January—and, after watching his inaugural address on TV, one friend remarked to me that she felt she understood the 'idea' of the US for the first time. Previously she had reacted against a perceived air of cultural superiority, an attitude of 'we know what's best for you, because we're the best'. Instead, she found she could now respect the idea of a nation built on principles of equality and liberty, even if those principles set such a high standard that any nation was bound to fail to live up to them as fully as they should.

In the UK, we are generally diffident, not to say anxious, about what 'nation' means. We may feel pulled in different directions, not keen on flag-waving jingoism but equally concerned not to lose all sense of who 'we' are and what values 'we' hold dear. In this issue of *Quiet Spaces*, we reflect on 'nation' in a variety of ways—what it means to belong to a group or a country but also how it feels to be different. We hear insights from the Church across the world, consider the particular issue of 'Celtic Christianity' and hear a poignant story of war-time experiences.

David Winter tells us a bit more about the patron saints of the UK—Andrew, George, Patrick and David—and suggests what we can draw from their stories to encourage us in our own walk of faith. And in an extract from his new book, *Confidence in the Living God*, Bishop Andrew Watson explores what a proper, godly confidence might look like, a confidence rooted in our Creator rather than simply in who we are or where we come from.

Naomi Starkey

1

Text copyright © BRF 2009
. uthors retain copyright in their own work
Illustrations copyright © Ian Mitchell, 2009
It has been impossible to trace copyright holders for some of the photographs reproduced here.
Further information is welcomed, and will result in full credit being given in any reprint.

Published by
The Bible Reading Fellowship
15 The Chambers, Vineyard
.\bingdon, OX14 3FE
United Kingdom
Tel: +44 (0)1865 319700
Email: enquiries@brf.org.uk
Website: www.brf.org.uk

ISBN 978 1 84101 600 9
First published 2009
10 9 8 7 6 5 4 3 2 1 0

Acknowledgments
Scripture quotations taken from The Holy Bible, New International Version, copyright © 1973, 1978, 1984 by International Bible Society, are used by permission of Hodder & Stoughton Publishers, a member of the Hachette Livre UK Group. All rights reserved. 'NIV' is a registered trademark of International Bible Society. UK trademark number 1448790.

Scripture quotations taken from The Holy Bible, Today's New International Version. Copyright © 2004 by International Bible Society. Used by permission of Hodder & Stoughton Publishers, a member of the Hachette Livre UK Group. All rights reserved. 'TNIV' is a registered trademark of International Bible Society.

Scripture quotations taken from The New Revised Standard Version of the Bible, Anglicised Edition, copyright (c) 1989, 1995 by the Division of Christian Education of the National Council of the Churches of Christ in the USA, and are used by permission. All rights reserved.

Extracts from the Authorised Version of the Bible (The King James Bible), the rights in which are vested in the Crown, are reproduced by permission of the Crown's patentee, Cambridge University Press.

A catalogue record for this book is available from the British Library

Printed by Gutenberg Press, Tarxien, Malta

Quiet Spaces

VOLUME 15

CONTENTS

Religious revival and nationalism in Russia

Canon Michael Bourdeaux is President of Keston Institute, Oxford. Over the last twelve years he has been co-editor of an encyclopedia on religion in Russia today in seven volumes, the final one of which has recently been published. He is widely consulted on religion in Russia.

Nashi—a recent buzz-word in the Russian press—sounds harsh to our ears, but it means simply 'ours'. It's the name of a government-funded youth movement, seen by many as a group of ultra-nationalist vigilantes who take the law into their own hands. The collapse of Communism in 1991 left a void in the Russian psyche, filled partly by an ugly form of nationalism, partly by a resurgence of the Russian Orthodox Church.

There are more than a few points in common between the two. Yet in past crises patriotism brought salvation. During three years of bitter struggle against the Nazi invasion of 1941, the Church, inspiring patriotism, became a force again after virtual extermination during Stalin's purges.

A religious revival began when the Soviet people were beaten to their knees. Stalin allowed, under strict conditions, the reopening of parish churches and the release of those imprisoned clergy who had survived the purges. As a reward for loyalty, he sanctioned the resumption of clergy training, realising at the same time that priests faithful to his policies could become propaganda agents, especially in the territories which fell under Soviet rule as a result of the westward thrust of the Red Army in the second half of the war.

Nikita Khrushchev shattered this *status quo* and let loose a further period of persecution in the early 1960s. All religions were affected, but

most notorious was the persecution of the Baptists. One group had been legal and recognised; another had refused to register, correctly claiming that this entailed state control. The story of their persecution shook—and divided—the Christian world from the 1960s to the 1980s, as some believed Soviet claims that they were being imprisoned only as miscreants who refused to accept Communist authority. Nothing much changed until 1985.

Then Mikhail Gorbachev, though an atheist, abolished restrictions on religion and introduced a new law in 1990, guaranteeing universal religious liberty. When change came, it was dramatic and led to the release of all political and religious prisoners. Lenin's ideology collapsed in 1991;

The collapse of Communism in 1991 left a void in the Russia psyche

all 15 Soviet republics went their own way, and three successive presidents of Russia—Boris Yeltsin, Vladimir Putin and Dmitri Medvedev—not only proclaimed themselves as believers but had the same agenda: to reinstate the authority of the Orthodox Church and bring it back centre stage. In this, the Kremlin's partner was Patriarch Alexi II, who died just short of his 80th birthday in 2008.

Russia today has other religions present in numbers: Muslims especially, but also Buddhists and

© Photos.com

... to reinstate the authority of the Orthodox Church

Jews, all of whom are now acknowledged as part of Russia's heritage. Yeltsin sanctioned a new law in 1997, however, which has been disastrous because it elevated the Russian Orthodox Church to a status above other Christian denominations —Catholics, Baptists, Lutherans and many others, which are not considered historically central to the main tradition. Under the 1997 law the 'minor' religions have to prove their historic existence—and to have been registered with the state—for a minimum of 15 years before they are accorded full legal rights. This may not sound too harsh a proviso, but when the law was brought in many had been outlawed under Communism. This affected the Roman Catholics especially, as their only legal church on Russian soil had been in Moscow.

The new law led to a temporary ban in Moscow on the ministry of the Salvation Army, even while they were doing admirable social work. However, fears of a systematic crackdown on Baptists and Catholics, as well as on the new religions, such as Scientology, the Moonies and Hare Krishna, were unfounded. Authoritarian and antidemocratic though Putin proved himself to be, open persecution of religious minorities is not on his agenda, nor could it be if he wishes to retain a modicum of his international reputation.

The Moscow Patriarchate (the governing body of the Russian Orthodox Church) uses its new freedom to act in as authoritarian a way as the Kremlin. Most bishops are antipathetic to other denominations, leading to endless disputes over the right of Protestants to build new churches and, with Catholics, to regain property confiscated after 1917.

Underlying all this is an ancient doctrine—that every national church has complete rights within its own 'canonical territory'. In the West, this did not survive the Reformation; in the East, it was more complicated. When the Orthodox churches evolved, they became identified with nationality. As well as the ancient Patriarchates of Jerusalem, Antioch and Constantinople, today there are newer ones in Russia, Romania, Bulgaria and Serbia. The rise of nationalism in the 19th century intensified the identification of religion and ethnicity, a situation complicated by Communist persecution. In recovering from this, the Russian Orthodox Church has turned its back on its contribution to the ecumenical movement from the 1960s to the 1980s and has tried to revert to the status it enjoyed before 1917. Psychologically, this is understandable; practically, it is disastrous.

The Orthodox Church claims the adherence of two thirds of Russia's 140 million people but much of this is nominal. The official sources of December 2008 state that the Moscow Patriarchate now has over 29,000 parish churches and 804 monasteries and convents, with new theological seminaries in most dioceses. Many of these churches are new, while others have been rebuilt from the ruins which Communism left behind. Best known is the new Cathedral of Christ the Saviour in central Moscow, erected on the site of the old cathedral, which was razed to the ground by Stalin before the war.

The heroic determination of parish priests and the financial sacrifices of the faithful have given civic pride back to countless local communities. I once saw Father Georgi Edelstein standing on top of a ladder, laying bricks with one hand despite a disability in the other, cementing them into the gap in a wall of his church in a country village 30 miles down an unmade road beyond Kostroma, 250 miles east of Moscow. The local mayor seconded a group of prisoners to work on the reconstruction. 'The state destroyed my church: you can help rebuild it,' Father Georgi told him.

The further we move away from parish life, the more authoritarianism predominates. The few Orthodox clergy who oppose the church — state symbiosis face severe criticism, even loss of livelihood. Bishops do not criticise Kremlin policy. The late Patriarch Alexi II blessed the Russian army on several occasions, most notably when it was about to descend on Chechnya, destroy Grozny, the capital, and beat the local people into submission. Orthodox priests recently sprinkled holy water on a new 'Triumph' surface-to-air missile. On 4 September 2007 the Patriarchate marked the 60th anniversary of the establishment of the Soviet nuclear arsenal with a 'thanksgiving' in the aforementioned Cathedral of Christ the Saviour. The building teemed with senior military personnel wearing badges in honour of St Serafim of Sarov, whose monastery is near Arzamas, a centre of the nuclear industry.

Sometimes it is the local bishop who acts as an agent of secular power. Sergei Taratukhin was imprisoned in the 1980s as a Soviet-era dissident. Fellow prisoners preached the gospel to him and he became a believer. He eventually trained for the priesthood and became chaplain in Penal Colony No. 10, near Chita in eastern Siberia. He served there for seven years, befriending an inmate, Mikhail Khodorkovsky, condemned by a Moscow court in 2005 for financial misdemeanours in a trial widely seen as politically motivated. Father Sergei became convinced that Khodorkovsky was indeed a political prisoner and campaigned for him. His diocesan bishop intervened and removed him to a remote parish. Father Sergei objected, so the bishop defrocked him. Now the priest has appeared abjectly contrite on television, in a scene grimly reminiscent of clergy recanting their anti-Soviet activities in former days. The bishop has offered him forgiveness and partial reinstatement: the priest now organises rubbish collections and shovels snow from the paths around Chita's new cathedral.

Father Pavel Adelheim was well known in the UK during his days as a political prisoner. He was so badly treated in prison that he lost a leg in an 'accident' and barely survived. Eventually, however, he was released and built up a parish in Pskov, notable for its social and educational work. He was about to acquire a building where 40 young people could train as church musicians when the bishop stepped in, unable to accept any unauthorised Christian work in his diocese. Last year Father Pavel was removed from his parish and has not been permitted

to work officially since.

There is a pattern here. Those who risked opposing the collaboration of the Orthodox Church with the state in Communist days have not become pillars of the church now it is free. Father Gleb Yakunin was perhaps the toughest pillar of opposition to Communist persecution. After long imprisonment he was elected deputy to the Duma in 1990, had privileged access to the KGB archives and discovered that the collaboration between some bishops and the state security agencies had been worse than even he had imagined. The church has never properly investigated this, clearly because so many of the bishops rose to power with the say-so of state authority.

There is a contrast in the Catholic Church. In Ukraine the 'Greek Catholic Church'—that is, the branch of Christendom using Slavonic for its liturgy and following the structures of the Orthodox Church (with married clergy and only monks permitted to become bishops)—was banned under Communism. Now it is back in a major way, following its re-legalisation late in the Gorbachev era. All its bishops had been imprisoned in 1946; those who survived eventually returned in triumph to reclaim the heritage that had been denied them by both Stalin and the Moscow Patriarchate. In the Roman Catholic Church in Lithuania, one young priest, Father Sigitas Tamkevičius, imprisoned for his defence of religious liberty, survived to become Archbishop of the ancient diocese of Kaunas.

Although the great leaders of Protestant opposition to Soviet atheist policy, Georgi Vins and Gennadi Kryuchkov, have died, both lived to experience the freedom for which they suffered so much. The schism with the registered Baptists went so deep that it has not been healed even today.

Mistakenly, millions of people in the West who prayed for and supported the persecuted church believed that the collapse of Communism signified that everything would immediately come right. As it was, during the 1990s, Christians in the West could do virtually anything to help Russian believers recoup the losses of almost three quarters of a century. Mistakes were made in abundance, however. Russia was not a mission field where there was no religion, but rather the opposite. Those who had endured the persecution had lessons in faith to offer the West, but there was little dialogue. Incoming missionaries offended the Orthodox Church by their patronising attitudes. There was an absence of coordinated policy in the West—in the religious sphere as in the political.

As in Soviet days, local initiatives can still be worthwhile and rewarding on both sides, congregation to congregation, but very little is being

© Galina Barskaya. Used under licence from Shutterstock, Inc.

done. To establish fellowship with Russia can never be easy. While there are always going to be language barriers, now many more Russians speak English than formerly. Visas for independent travel are expensive but not impossible to obtain. As previously, you cannot do anything unless you know the facts and therefore know where to begin. Once again, the need is to be informed and to back this up with prayer. Putin's policies may seem hostile to the West, but when you meet Russians face to face, they are still the most open and friendly people in the world. ∎

Keston Institute produces a quarterly *Newsletter* to inform readers of developments in Russia (sample copies from PO Box 752, Oxford OX1 9QF or admin@keston.org.uk). Membership of Keston is £25 per annum (£5 for students). There is also a website: www.keston.org.uk.

The Search for
Celtic Christianity

Thomas O'Loughlin is Professor of Historical Theology at the University of Nottingham. He previously held a similar role in the University of Wales, Lampeter. His research concentrates on how Christians in the early centuries of the Church used their memories to give expression to their faith in changing cultural situations.

The desire to tap into what are seen as the 'riches' of 'Celtic Christianity' is one of the significant themes of contemporary English-speaking spirituality. The ill-defined past of 'the Celtic Christians' is perceived to offer forms of church life that are less authoritarian, less rationalist, more sensitive to nature and its rhythms and to creativity and women's insights. For others, it offers a pre-Reformation unity to legitimate practices, like pilgrimage, that might otherwise be rejected as 'High Church'.

In stark contrast is the reaction of historians to these claims. First, 'Celtic' is a linguistic rather than a social category. Second, the churches in those areas are not different in theology from those bordering them, and differences similar to those that do occur can be found across the Latin West. Third, the language of those churches was Latin, and they saw themselves, albeit in a looser manner, as linked with Rome: they prayed for the Pope at every Eucharist. Fourth, they interacted with the other Western churches in Spain, France and Italy. Finally, their sensitivity to nature's rhythms was normal in pre-industrial societies.

While critics often present 'Celtic Christianity' as a fraud, that ignores the fact that Christians continually recycle parts of their past for present needs. The question we should pose is not 'Was there a Celtic Christianity?' or even 'What does Celtic Christianity mean today?' but rather 'What areas of Christian practice today are challenged or inspired by recalling the thoughts and behaviour of long ago?' These early Christians in the British

Isles lived in a world vastly different from ours, but we are strangely connected with them because they occupied the same places we occupy; because of our shared space, they seem close. Reflecting on those early insular Christians can challenge us in at least two respects.

Times and seasons

People living before the Industrial Revolution, and especially before the Agricultural Revolution that made it possible, had a very different attitude to times and seasons. Inherent in our notion of time is the idea that time's 'uses' can be pre-programmed. Indeed, we can buy and sell 'time', whether it is for fun (minutes on the phone), for parking (the ticket shows how much you have bought), or for business (experts charge by fractions of an hour). Funnily enough, when time is so carefully parcelled out, we seem never to have enough of it. Moreover, what we want most is 'time off'. This 'time off'—the time we need for ourselves, others, relaxation, restoration—is then seen as not really time at all. Living in this sort of cosmos means that we are always under pressure. Time for friends, for reflection, for prayer and for 'just being' seems to slip ever further away. Meanwhile, we determine that nothing should get in our way of imposing our plans on time: anything from the weather to a bereavement upsetting the schedule is a 'disruption'.

We are strangely connected with them

When we read books such as the monastic allegory known as *The Journey of St Brendan*, we are struck by a completely different way of experiencing time. The monks have a rhythm that is based on the rising and setting of the sun, and that changes over the year's seasons. Prayer and meals set the day's markers, and work is fitted around them; yet the monks drop all of these and run to greet a visitor from another monastery.

When we read such documents we might be filled with a romantic longing to live in that 'simple' way, but it is an illusion. However, if that document sets a question mark over our lifestyle and reminds us that our attitude to time is not an absolute, then reading that ancient monastic text has served us.

It is November as I write: winter's cold darkness has arrived, but the supermarket has fresh fruit, vegetables and meat from every season and from across the globe. At home I have automatic light and heat: I am isolated from the seasons. I dare not think how much of the earth's resources are expended to give me this comfort, and I become so blasé regarding choices that I forget to be thankful to God for any of it. If I cannot feel the physical year, then what hope have I of entering into the mysteries through the liturgical year?

Once again, when we read texts such as saints' lives, we sense the constant background melody of the seasons, natural and liturgical. We may find the formulae and miracles of these lives somewhat akin to seeing an array of gaudily painted baroque statues. But their unconscious insistence on the seasons, thankfulness for food, their awareness that food must be produced locally or there will be starvation, and the sense that 'for everything there is a season, and a time for every matter under heaven' (Ecclesiastes 3:1, NRSV) is striking. Again we must guard against romantic hindsight, but we might do well to be re-sensitised to the fragility of the earth, to living as creatures within a universe that is ordered by

being made through the Word, and to our need to offer thanks. As that ancient grace, used in Celtic lands, expressed it: 'For these gifts we are about to eat which come to us from thy generosity through Christ our Lord.'

A common loaf and cup

Anyone attending an average Eucharist on a Sunday—the experience varies a little between denominations—could easily imagine that they are attending a short Bible study session with another ceremony tacked on, which ends with the acceptance of a sacred token: a nibble of bread and a sip of wine! Modern eucharistic practice is full of contradictions. On the theoretical side, theologians and church leaders argue about what it 'means'—and in the process turn the very heart of Christian unity into a source for reinforcing division. On the practical side, pastors tell people of the gathering's significance—but the actual event seems far less than the meal that imitates all those welcoming meals of Jesus with his followers. Nor does it seem to express the bonds that make us companions, literally 'table sharers', as Christians today, and nor does it feel like an anticipation of the banquet of heaven!

In fact, the sacred meal of the Lord has become a sign of a sign of a sign: what we actually do is but a pointer to what we should be doing in celebrating the Lord's Supper, and that real celebration of the Lord's Supper is a pointer to the mystical Banquet. Meanwhile, on Sunday in some communities it will only be a tiny piece of 'bread' that is 'given out'; in many this will be 'unleavened' (the opposite of a sign of life and joy); for many these token 'breads' will be pre-cut (the opposite of sharing in a broken loaf); in some places these wafers will be the 'afters' from an earlier celebration (hardly the image of a feast). The wine will be just a sip and sometimes given in a glass thimble to avoid the shocking demands of the Lord's symbolism that, as Christians, we are prepared to share a single cup with one another and with him.

What this has to do with Celtic practices is that by looking at such objects as the cup and paten from Derrynaflan in Ireland, we can see the earlier practices, while in their liturgical texts we can read how their practice of sharing a single loaf and cup was interpreted theologically. Both cup and paten were intended for a community of fewer than a hundred people and assumed that each had a regular mouthful of wine from the cup and a decent-sized piece of bread from the loaf. The cup holds 1.5 litres of wine, and the loaf was at least 30cm in diameter. Moreover, this paten followed the then canonical requirements: the loaf had to be one round object (indicating unity), fresh and white (indicating that it should be the best bread available), and living (in other words, leavened, for it would

> **Our attitude to time is not an absolute**

become the loaf of the Living One). It was then broken up, according to an elaborate ritual, and each had his/her share.

Recalling the practice that animated the buildings whose ruins we still visit today can serve to remind us that we Western Christians are still obsessed with the late-medieval disputes that sparked the divisions of the Reformation. Those disputes led to the Eucharist being almost irrelevant for many Christians (who have become Bible-obsessed) and a source of conflict for other Christians (obsessed with technical theological debates). When those Christians around AD800 heard, 'The cup of blessing that we bless, is it not a sharing in the blood of Christ? The bread that we break, is it not a sharing in the body of Christ? Because there is one bread, we who are many are one body, for we all partake of the one bread' (1 Corinthians 10:16–17); they could see and taste that reality on Sunday!

Christians are always remembering and always forgetting. Recalling the practice and thought of our sisters and brothers who have gone before us, and who once lived in the very places where we live now, can be a mirror to us showing where we need to change and grow. ■

Global
Communion

Jane Williams is a lecturer at the St Paul's Theological Centre in London and also works part-time for Redemptorist Publications. She has written six books, including 'Marriage, Mitres and Being Myself' (SPCK, 2008), and is married with two children.

The Lambeth Conference has been happening every ten years since 1867. Occasionally, as during the First and Second World Wars, the date has shifted slightly, but the principle remains. It offers an opportunity for the leaders of the global Anglican Church to meet together and take counsel.

It is, I think, significant that Archbishops of Canterbury began to call Lambeth Conferences at a time when the Anglican Church was growing fast and becoming much more multicultural. By the middle of the 19th century, the Anglican Church was established in many countries and had become genuinely local. It was no longer just the English taking their religion with them abroad. Although at that very first Lambeth Conference many of the bishops were still Englishmen, their priests and congregations were not. Now, of course, each Province of the Anglican Church is deeply rooted in its own context. One of the greatest pleasures of the Lambeth Conference in 2008 was to have worship led by each of the Provinces. The shape of the

Eucharist, for example, was recognisably the same, and yet so transformed by different styles of music, dancing, vestments and symbolism.

It was part of my role to help plan the Conference for the spouses of bishops—we are spouses, now, not just wives, as there are a number of women bishops. The fact that we wanted to make sure that everybody who came was welcomed and appropriately heard presented a huge challenge because of our cultural diversity. There were little things, like the fact that in some cultures it is unheard of for a woman to sleep in a room on her own. She would have grown up sleeping in a room with sisters and, when married, would expect to share a room with husband and children. The centre we stayed at in Canterbury

© Lambeth Conference

... transformed by different styles of music, dancing, vestments and symbolism

was set up for the British conference trade, with single study-bedrooms. Food was an issue—in this country we have too much of it, on a regular basis, and that is appalling and disgraceful to many of our visitors, who see bins bulging with food and think of children starving at home.

There were also, of course, communication challenges, which didn't just mean providing teams and teams of translators, though it did mean that. It also meant giving attention to how we learn from

We knew that we were 'family' and could talk with honesty and be heard with prayer

each other, and when it was acceptable to challenge and question, and when it was not. It is very easy to give offence across cultures through sheer ignorance, and the only way to avoid it is to be open about how little we know of each other, and learn to listen better, with our ears, with our eyes, with our hearts.

All of this was an education in itself, but it was not what the Conference was for. It was only what made the Conference possible.

One of the things the Conference was designed for was to enable the leaders to look together at the tasks that face us. All of us share in the problems and opportunities that arise from climate change, from living alongside people of other faiths and no faith, from the AIDS pandemic, from globalisation of markets and so on. These are issues where church leaders can learn from each other and share experiences and resources, so that we can better serve God's people, both inside and outside the Church.

The Conference also enabled us to hear what it is really like to live and work and follow Jesus in different countries. We heard directly from church leaders in Pakistan, in Australia, in Myanmar, in the US, in Congo, in Brazil, in Scotland, in Melanesia—the list goes on and on. I am still breathless with the sense of privilege. Where else could I have had the opportunity of spending time with such a mix of people? And it was not just superficial time—it was deep time. We started with so much in common, because of our faith and our commitment to its expression in the Anglican Church. We were able to cut through the small talk and get straight to a powerful telling of our own stories. We knew that we were 'family' and could talk with honesty and be heard with prayer.

On the basis of those weeks together, all of us returned to our own contexts equipped to be advocates for one another. I can tell people here of some of the heroic witness of the church in Myanmar, or of the work being done with street children and prostitutes in India, or how the bishops' wives in the Congo are ministering to the many, many women who have been horrifically raped in that country's fighting. And they, in turn, can go home and witness that there really are Christians in England or America, and that we are not all spiritually and morally dead. Connections of prayer, emotional support and material help have been made

© Lambeth Conference

... to be open about how little we know of each other, and **learn to listen better**

We are God's gift to each other

or restored at every level, from personal friendships, through diocesan links to all the inter-Anglican networks.

All of this was vital work, but undergirding it was something just as important. The Conference gave us a chance to reflect upon ourselves as Church so that we can better fulfil our calling as disciples and witnesses of Jesus Christ. The good news is the same in all cultures, but every single culture needs to learn that. We all need to learn that Jesus is not only to be found and followed in the ways that are familiar to us.

There is a thread running throughout the New Testament that is about the extraordinary, breathtaking, miraculous newness of the community that is created through God's coming in Christ. 1 Peter 2 calls us 'a royal priesthood, a holy nation, God's own people... Once you were not a people, but now you are God's people.' (vv. 9–10, NRSV). Ephesians 2 says, 'So then you are no longer strangers and aliens, but you are citizens with the saints and also members of the household of God' (v. 19). In John 17, Jesus prays that all his disciples may be one, 'so that the world may know that you have sent me and have loved them even as you have loved me' (v. 23). I could go on.

We are not Christians and churchgoers because it suits us or because we like the lifestyle but because God, in his graciousness, called us. We don't have a choice about who else God calls, and whether we like them and agree with them or not. We are not the hosts; we do not make this community, the Church; we are God's gift to each other, like it or not. Only together, in our variety, in our differences, can we begin to glimpse something of God's new creation.

The bold hope is that the Church is actually called to be a microcosm of the redeemed human race. In tiny glimpses at the Lambeth Conference, during worship, or when I saw two women from different countries weeping and hugging each other, or groups of people from all over the world laughing and singing together, or gathered in silent reverence around the cross—the symbol of God's costly love that brings his new people to birth—in those tiny glimpses, I was not just seeing the Anglican Church as it should be but the human race as it should be. We are meant to be one family; there are things about ourselves, our world and our God that we can learn only together, from one another, and that is not an accident—it is because that is how our Creator made us.

I do not wish to pretend that the Anglican Communion is now perfect. It is not. But I came away from Canterbury immensely heartened and inspired, and, above all, humbled. God's gift to us, the gift of one another, is glorious beyond imagining, and it can be shared by everyone. ■

All of us returned to our own contexts **equipped to be advocates for one another**

© Lambeth Conference

A journey to
understanding

Sylvia Diamond is married to a vicar (now retired), has a grown-up family and grandchildren, and has taught English and written for children. In recent years she has enjoyed giving English support to overseas students at theological colleges.

One warm summer's day I was walking with my husband through Bad Wurzach, a quiet little spa town in the gentle, green countryside of southern Germany. It was not an unusual time or place for a holiday but, unusually, we were being led by the *Bürgermeister*, the town's mayor, towards the imposing 18th-century *Schloss*; and, even more unusually, the great doors were being opened especially for us. The reason was that I had once unwillingly lived there.

As we approached, I struggled with memories of a grim, grey building surrounded by barbed wire and patrolled by armed soldiers and fierce Alsatian dogs. Here were colourful, cheerful gardens, where I remembered a bare compound, iron-hard from soldiers' boots. But, chillingly familiar, the same guardhouses were still there at the gates. My last view of those gates had been when they were flung open for American lorries to tear through in June 1945, as they carried away the *Schloss*'s thankful ex-inmates. After two years and nine months, over 600 men, women and children were going home.

Home was the island of Jersey, peaceful and untroubled until the fall of France in 1940 and subsequently occupied by German forces. Enemy occupation of one's beloved homeland is a terrible

theft of freedom but the people had to adjust. They dug vegetable gardens and kept rabbits to survive and quietly resisted whenever possible. Resistance could be minor, like my mother's pushing the pram as hard as possible across a soldier's feet when the poor homesick man had wanted to admire her baby and toddler. Some, like my uncle, hid wireless sets, so that BBC news could still be relayed to islanders cut off from the outside world. The bravest hid Russian slave workers trying to escape their appalling treatment.

Then my father quietly resisted, altering the course of our war. In September 1942, Hitler decided that anyone not born in the islands should be deported, together with their families. All my family were

I struggled with memories of a grim, grey building surrounded by barbed wire and patrolled by armed soldiers

Then my father quietly resisted, altering the course of our war

More painful memories surfaced

Jersey-born except my father. A German soldier knocked on the door and showed our names on the list: William, Alice, Patricia and Sylvia Butler. We were to leave the next day.

The news spread like wildfire. Immediately my mother's family offered to care for my sister and me, aged four and two-and-a-half, should my parents gain permission to leave us behind. My father raced to town and gained an appointment with the island's *Kommandant*. He seemed to listen sympathetically and then offered to exempt my parents as well, on condition that my father agreed to work for the Germans. I doubt whether Dad had a scripture verse in mind at that moment but he did know that if he complied, he would 'lose his soul'. So next day we stood among hundreds of others at the harbour with one suitcase each, our distraught families unsure whether they would ever see us again.

A long, hot train journey and several weeks in a transit camp led us eventually to Wurzach. Originally built for the local Grand Duke, Wurzach Schloss had become a run-down prison, infested with fleas and lice. Jersey housewives quickly began their own war—against grime, scrubbing filthy floors with half-bricks and attacking germs with my mother's little bottle of Jeyes Fluid.

Now, all those years later, as we approached the familiar façade of this restored castle, the huge doors swung open and we gasped at a riot of colour. Wartime dirt must have hidden the exuberant gods and cherubs of classical myths that adorned the walls and ceiling of the Great Hall. But now my own childhood memories rushed to the surface. That grand stone staircase was where we children would race down to the compound—sometimes with empty Red Cross tins, to fill with snow and take back to the hot pipes that skirted our room, just to watch it melt. Our first science lesson!

We climbed the stairs. Where was the long corridor which had been our playground, the doorless cupboards ideal for hide-and-seek? Above

all, where was Room 56? That long room contained my earliest memories—high windows down one side, bare wooden floors and a large iron stove in the centre. Close together around the walls were double bunk beds with straw mattresses, a small rough table and bench in front of each. My mother, sister and I shared one bottom bunk, someone else above. This room became home for 36 women and children.

Sadly, it now lay in the private quarters of the Jesuit priests who live in the building today. We did find my father's dormitory, though. The men had been separated from us but allowed to join their families during the day. They had organised committees to care for every aspect of camp life, with German-speakers liaising with the guards. A little school was started with few materials but even fewer distractions, so we infants were fluent readers by the age of five! I treasured and read hundreds of times two illustrated books sent from an American Catholic organisation—cheerful, homely stories with a Christian basis.

Nightmares featuring soldiers and tanks continued through my childhood

I believe that prompting, when it came, was from the heart of God

We reached a room which had been 'hospital', where more painful memories surfaced. My father had contracted diphtheria. Then scarlet fever arrived and I remembered lying isolated and very ill in this room, cared for by Jersey nurses and a kind German doctor. Red Cross parcels saved our lives.

My memories were a jumble of snapshots, some happy in the love of our parents and the kindness of friends, others fearful. The shock of the deportation caused my sister to stop speaking—'elective mutism'. It took months of care and coaxing by my parents to get her to speak again. I was terrified by the dogs and this fear has stayed with me into adulthood. We had watched from those high windows as my father and others rolled out huge POW letters in the compound, because of the fear of being bombed by Allied planes in the closing months of the war. Sirens sounded but they disobeyed the order to go inside—and we saw a guard point his rifle at them. Nightmares featuring soldiers and tanks continued through my childhood.

After the war, gratitude that we had survived, while so many other lives had been shattered, buried the memories. As an American nurse, caring for us on the journey home, had said to my mother, with tears, 'Thank God, my dear, that you were not Jewish!' Later, in a busy life of teaching, married to a vicar and bringing up four children, it had never occurred to me to go back. I believe that prompting, when it came, was from the heart of God.

It began when our elder son fell in love with a German girl! This was no problem. We had enjoyed working with many nationalities when at the L'Abri community in Switzerland. But when I found her home town on the map it seemed uncomfortably close to Wurzach, and my stomach tightened. Were there unhealed memories? They chose the second Saturday in May for their wedding—9 May, celebrated in the Channel Islands since 1945 as Liberation Day. Was God saying something? As I prayed about it, two unexpected invitations arrived, one to our daughter-in-law's home near the Black

Forest, the second to Switzerland, near Lake Constance. Wurzach is 40 miles north of the lake. An amazing door was opening. I decided to write to the *Bürgermeister*.

The mayor's welcome could not have been warmer or more understanding. I discovered that Wurzach, always synonymous with 'prison camp' in my mind, had become a spa town where people went to bathe away their aches and pains in the mineral waters—a healing place. The prison itself had become a Jesuit-run home for the elderly and disabled—another healing place. I was aware of a similar process taking place in me, but I needed to make one more visit to complete it. At the village church I was struck by the memorial boards that filled the porch walls. One listed all the Wurzach men killed in the war. The other contained an even longer list of those simply missing—lost on the Russian front? So many, from such a little place!

© Dr A. Raichle

a healing place

We went to visit the graves of the 13 Jersey people who had died in the camp. They were beautifully kept, bordered with flowers. Nearby a fine memorial recorded the Jersey names alongside the lost Wurzach men—the fathers, sons, husbands, brothers. They had probably wanted this war as little as we had and had suffered grievously. My heart went out in sympathy, and in that peaceful, sunny garden my remembered fears were banished and a weight was lifted as a new understanding dawned. I found myself remembering the titles of my treasured camp books: *These Are Our Friends* and *These Are Our Neighbours*. ∎

Jersey and Bad Wurzach were officially reconciled in 2002 when a document twinning the town with St Helier was signed both in Jersey and in the castle where islanders had been imprisoned. There are now frequent cultural and sporting exchanges and ties of friendship.

A stranger in a foreign land

Amy Boucher Pye works with words from the vicarage home in north London that she shares with her husband, two small children, German au pair and heaving shelves of books. A US American, she hasn't adopted a British accent but does enjoy pronouncing 'advertisement' in the British style. She writes for various publications, including 'New Daylight', 'Day by Day with God' and 'Inspiring Women Every Day'.

I lost my confidence when I moved to the UK a dozen years ago. I changed from Amy Boucher, a single professional who lived in DC and had a thriving social network, to Mrs Pye, a name previously reserved only for my mother-in-law. In the blink of an eye and the declaring of marital vows, I had transported my world from one side of the Atlantic to the other. In doing so I didn't realise that I had also turned it upside down.

When we arrived at Heathrow I was dazed with jetlag and exhaustion. As we drove from the airport to our new home, I had a moment of revelation: this was now my country. I was no longer just an American, but an American living in Britain. I wondered what that would mean, and the thought came to me from a wise English woman who had lived in Washington, DC for many years: 'Now, dear, you will have one toe on each side of the pond.'

In that moment I also felt God's reassuring promise that he would never leave me. The words from Ruth flashed into my mind, 'Where you go I will go, and where you stay I will stay. Your people will be my people and your God my God' (Ruth 1:16, TNIV). This I had promised to my husband in our marriage vows, and this I would live out, with God's help.

Nicholas was in his final year at theological college in Cambridge, and we were living in college accommodation aptly named the White House. But it was far from Pennsylvania Avenue in the beloved city I had just left. Yet my new husband told me that American soil was just up the road, at the American cemetery. If I could cycle up a huge hill, I could glimpse the Stars and Stripes.

We got to our tiny flat and started unpacking. I was eager to email loved ones back home, so one of the first things I assembled was my desktop computer. And that's when I had my first shock at one of the differences of life in England: electrical voltage. Yes, I blew my computer by not realising it had a little button signifying 110 or 220 volts.

I was no longer just an American, but **an** American living in Britain

Gone was my lifeline to all that was familiar

Gone was communication. Gone was my lifeline to all that was familiar. Gone was my independence. To the fore came floods of tears as I felt stripped and pushed down.

Reverting to adolescence

George Bernard Shaw has famously said that the UK and US are two countries separated by a common language, and I felt I was living this disjointed existence every day. For instance, I knew it wasn't a 'parking lot' but I couldn't remember that it was a 'car park'. Although I knew some pronunciations were different, such as 'aluminum' or 'advertisement', I was thrown when I heard 'oregano' and 'schedule'. And I was stumped when I tried to describe a garbage truck. A dust cart? I'm still mystified.

Not being sure of the correct words dented my confidence, as did being newly married and unemployed.

What was my purpose? What did it matter if I watched old movies all day long? No one was expecting anything from me. It seemed that I had turned into a small and helpless child.

Or perhaps I had become an adolescent, for I became painfully self-conscious about being a foreigner. When I went into a shop I was aware that if I didn't speak I wouldn't be seen as different, so I often kept mum. After a dozen years here I've thankfully lost this over-awareness, but I'm still always described as 'the American' and just yesterday a woman at Tesco's commented on my 'lovely accent' (yes, really!)

My computer crash was the start of a difficult period of adjustment to life in the UK. I, too, came crashing down on the first day of moving here. I was not to enjoy the honeymoon period that many new arrivals have, when everything is exciting, fresh and amazing. I was delighted finally to be married and I knew I was supposed to be here, but I was still miserable.

Foreigners and strangers on earth

When Nicholas and I were contemplating marriage, we each went on a quiet retreat to pray and seek God's guidance about the potential union. I finished mine on the Fourth of July, and later joined the throngs celebrating their independence with fireworks, food and friends on the Mall in Washington, DC. But in the morning I was in rural Maryland and was reading about Abraham, that stranger who lived in a foreign country. The text of Hebrews 11 was coming clear to me in an amazing yet frightening way, for I felt that I, too, was being called to a new land.

As Nicholas was studying to be a vicar, I knew that I would need to be the one to leave my family, friends, work, church and good plumbing behind as we melded our lives together. But until that retreat, I hadn't considered the deeper implications of what such a move might entail.

I hadn't noticed before that Abraham was *obedient* in going to this new place: 'By faith Abraham, when called to go to a place he would later receive as his inheritance, obeyed and went, even though he did not know where he was going' (Hebrews 11:8). In the flush of the first stages of romantic love, it didn't seem a hardship to be obedient to a move to a foreign land. I was then blissfully unaware of the costs involved, and the obedience would need to come later in accepting, with grace and without bitterness or complaining, what I had signed up to.

Like Abraham, I didn't know where we were going; Cambridge was the first stop, but that would be for just seven months while Nicholas finished his studies before ordination. I didn't know then that I would be moving four times in five years and thus would be a wanderer like Abraham, who lived in tents (v. 9). This moving brought upheavals and uprootedness, but over time God answered my pleas for comfort, a few girlfriends and even a fabulous job.

On that Independence Day the thing that struck me so deeply was that I was leaving my earthly citizenship behind. I would be a 'foreigner and stranger' (v. 13) and would therefore need to claim my heavenly citizenship. Like the heroes of faith listed in Hebrews 11, I would be looking for a country of my own, a 'better country—a heavenly one' (v. 16). I would have my US American passport, and eventually would claim a British one, but my heavenly passport would denote my defining identity.

I was leavng my **earthly citizenship behind**

My confidence has been strengthened as I keep my hand firmly clasped in his

Longing for eternity

The greatest longing and ache of living on this small island is the separation from my family and friends. When I left, my niece was four and my nephew was two; now they are teenagers and I've missed much of their formative years. My parents are active and healthy, but I realised recently with a start that they won't be around for ever. When I'm missing them I'll either pick up the phone (if it's not their middle of the night) or remind myself that we'll have eternity together when God himself will dwell with us.

Living here has brought me an abundance of blessings. Some include cultural and historical delights, a new appreciation for the monarchy through a five-year-old who is wild about Queen Victoria, access to a really good curry, the excitement of Wimbledon. I have an instant connection with others who are living as ex-pats. Having been immersed in the culture, I can better understand British authors, such as C.S. Lewis. I have left behind a trail of power showers for other clergy families, although I haven't always been able to introduce mixer taps.

I still have bewildering and jetlagged trips from Heathrow, like the one last week when the taxi driver went to Terminal 3 instead of Terminal 1, where I sat with two exhausted children, car seats, suitcases and a travel cot spewed around me. But my confidence has been strengthened as I keep my hand firmly clasped in his who walked this earth 2000 years ago and who gives us love, empathy, grace and peace as we enjoy the adventure together. ■

Confidence in the
Living God

Christians are called to proclaim their faith in the living God, but how can we build this confidence in a culture where such faith is often dismissed as embarrassing at best? This is an extract from 'Confidence in the Living God' (BRF, 2009), in which Andrew Watson interweaves reflections on the story of David and Goliath with insights about God's ability to develop a proper self-confidence within individuals and his Church.

In a very real sense it is confidence which lies at the very heart of the market economy, confidence which determines the success or failure of every human institution, and confidence which makes the lives of individuals either positive and resilient or painful and resigned. Confidence in the leadership and vision of a school, business or political party is a central factor in the rise or fall of the entire enterprise.

Confidence in the FTSE index and the housing and money markets wholly dictates the monetary value of companies and property, and even the monetary value of money itself! Confidence in an interview plays a major, often decisive, part in the wording of the letter which arrives on the doormat a few days later.

What, though, does the word 'confidence' really mean, and how do we recognise it in an individual or an institution?

The Latin from which our English word is derived (*con fide*) means 'with faith', and suggests that confident people both have faith in themselves and inspire the faith of others: hence their frequent successes in the interview room and around the boardroom table. That faith may well be misplaced or misguided: it is quite possible for individuals or institutions to be confident and incompetent, or even confident and corrupt. That faith may be self-serving and off-putting. But where it is combined with ability, integrity and modesty, there is something about this gift of confidence which is both attractive and inspiring. Confident people have a sureness of step, whatever the complexities of modern-day living. Confident institutions know where they're going, whatever the challenges they encounter along the way.

The biblical languages add something to this understanding. The root of the Hebrew word most often translated 'confidence' (*beTach*) has the sense of being open, of having nothing to hide (so stressing the integrity theme), while two Greek words, *parrhesia* and *pepoithesis*, convey a sense of assurance, trust and boldness. A third Greek word, *hupostasis*, means literally something 'set under' something else, hence a foundation. When the author of the letter to the Hebrews writes, 'We have come to share in Christ if we hold firmly till the end the confidence we had at first' (3:14, NIV), his use of the word *hupostasis* suggests that the Church's original confidence in Christ is foundational, and is therefore able to endure the toughest of challenges and temptations.

For the Christian believer, though, and for those from other religious backgrounds, this sense of faith and trust inevitably raises the issue of where that faith and trust are to be placed. We may not be too familiar with the unnamed field commander of Sennacherib, king of Assyria, but the question he asks of Hezekiah,

king of Judah, remains both pertinent and searching: 'On what are you basing this confidence of yours?' (2 Kings 18:19). (This incident is also recorded in 2 Chronicles 32 and Isaiah 36.)

In response to the question, there is a common and apparently straightforward theme throughout the scriptures (and one with which Hezekiah most clearly concurred) that we are to place our confidence in God: 'You have been my hope, O Sovereign Lord, my confidence since my youth' (Psalm 71:5). In the New Testament this is combined with a sense of awe that through Christ we can 'approach the throne of grace with confidence, so that we may receive mercy and find grace to help us in our time of need' (Hebrews 4:16). The curtain in the temple has been torn from top to bottom, and the writer to the Hebrews marvels at the 'new and living way' into God's presence brought about through the death of Jesus who is both sacrifice and great high priest (see 10:19–22).

If the Lord is to be our confidence—and if the same Lord can be confidently approached—the foolishness of placing our confidence in anything (or anyone) else is self-evident, and this again forms a common and apparently straightforward biblical theme: 'Egypt will no longer be a source of confidence for the people of Israel but will be a reminder of their sin in turning to her for help' (Ezekiel 29:16). That doesn't mean that we are called to mistrust all human beings, including our nearest and dearest: the husband of the exemplary wife in Proverbs 31 'has full confidence in her and lacks nothing of value' (v. 11), while Paul, writing to the troublesome church at Corinth, emphasises (perhaps a little too often!) how he has 'complete confidence' in them (2 Corinthians 7:16; see also 2:3; 3:4; 7:4; 8:22). But when it comes to the very foundations of our lives—our deepest security as human beings—there is no question that God alone is to be trusted, and we are to accept no cheap imitations.

There are at least two issues which remain unresolved in such an approach, however, and the first and most obvious is the question of where it leaves *self*-confidence. Self-confidence, after all, is generally what most people mean whenever they use the 'c' word in relation to an acquaintance, friend or colleague. But is it a virtue or a vice when it comes to the Christian believer?

At first sight it would appear that confidence in God excludes a confidence in ourselves, that the two simply cannot coexist. In Philippians 3, after all, Paul writes of the dangers of putting 'confidence in the flesh', and emphatically considers all his worldly advantages as so much 'garbage' compared with the 'surpassing worth of knowing Christ Jesus my Lord' (v. 8). Christian doctrine relating to sin, humility and self-denial hardly sits easily with

secular teaching on confidence and self-esteem; and as a result many Christians are reticent in response to this theme, regularly acknowledging the dangers of living 'in my own strength' and stressing (with the prophet Isaiah) that all their righteous acts are like 'filthy rags' (64:6).

There is another side to this argument, though—one which allows for the possibility that confidence in God and a proper self-confidence are much more closely related than we sometimes think. A useful analogy might perhaps be drawn with the question of whether our love for God diminishes or excludes all other loves, for while it's true that Jesus uses a graphic Jewish idiom to emphasise that nothing should compete with our primary relationship with him (Luke 14:26), the call to 'love one another' (and even the assumption that we love ourselves: Matthew 22:38–39; compare Ephesians 5:29) could hardly be stronger in the Gospels or the New Testament as a whole. Might there, then, be a parallel situation when it comes to confidence, a sense in which our confidence in God (and in the gifts, abilities and life experiences with which he has entrusted us) can enhance, not eclipse, a proper confidence in ourselves? It is an intriguing question, and one to which we will return later in the book. ■

Music for the soul:
Land of Hope and Glory

Gordon Giles is vicar of St Mary Magdalene's Church, Enfield, north London. He contributes to BRF's 'New Daylight' notes and has also written four books for BRF, including the Lent book 'Fasting and Feasting' (2008).

*Dear Land of Hope, thy hope is
    crowned,
God make thee mightier yet!
On Sov'ran brows, beloved, renowned,
Once more thy crown is set.
Thine equal laws, by Freedom gained,
Have ruled thee well and long;
By Freedom gained, by Truth
    maintained,
Thine Empire shall be strong.
Land of Hope and Glory, Mother of the
    Free,
How shall we extol thee, who are born
    of thee?
Wider still and wider shall thy bounds
    be set;
God, who made thee mighty, make thee
    mightier yet,
God, who made thee mighty, make thee
    mightier yet.
Thy fame is ancient as the days,
As Ocean large and wide:
A pride that dares, and heeds not
    praise,*

*A stern and silent pride;
Not that false joy that dreams content
With what our sires have won;
The blood a hero sire hath spent
Still nerves a hero son.*

WORDS: A.C. BENSON (1862–1925)
MUSIC: 'POMP AND CIRCUMSTANCE' MARCH
NO 1, BY EDWARD ELGAR (1857–1934)

Nowadays nationalism is a kind of secret vice: we are all supposed to be in a globalised, economically interdependent, multi-faith, international culture. On the other hand one does not have to make a massive fuss about the evils of political correctness to enjoy a bit of patriotic singing.

'Land of Hope and Glory' and 'Jerusalem' are not only as popular as ever at The Last Night of the Proms, but both songs (they are hardly 'hymns'!) are among the few of which people actually know the lyrics. And

The idea of nation **doesn't make sense without God**

there is nothing quite like a vast crowd all singing from the same song sheet! This, of course, is partly why the 'Last Night' remains so popular, for it has managed to hold on to a tradition of musical fellowship, creating what we might call a form of secular worship.

Patriotic song-singing may invoke God, not out of respect or gratitude, but merely as a ploy in self-elevation. Nationalism can involve praise of self, of monarch, of an ideal, land or nation. Whatever 'nation' is, at its worst it involves division of humanity, self-glorification and judgmentalism. But this negative view obscures much that can be good: family ties, mutual value, fellowship, unity and celebration. The idea of nation doesn't make sense without God. For it is God who makes us diverse, as individuals and peoples, and from the Bible we know that God both creates and affirms the diversity of his world: 'God saw everything that he had made, and indeed, it was very good.' (Genesis 1:31, NRSV). The very idea of nationhood is God-given: Abraham is promised that God will make a nation of him (Genesis 12:2), but the purpose of nationhood is to give coherence to diversity, not to promote enmity. Thus there can be a respectable, even desirable form of nationalism, which associates

nationality with God, recognising the debt of gratitude we owe to God for our health, wealth and peace.

'Land of Hope and Glory' does not immediately present itself as a candidate for God-affirming Christian gatherings. Yet its author was the son of an Archbishop of Canterbury and Master of Magdalene College, Cambridge, where the music performance room is still named after him. Arthur Christopher Benson's father, Edward White Benson (1829–96), was headmaster of Wellington College when Arthur was born but later became the first Bishop of Truro and then Archbishop of Canterbury in 1883. Arthur's poetry gained unofficial recognition from Queen Victoria, and he wrote 'Land of Hope and Glory' as a coronation ode for King Edward VII in 1902, with Elgar's first 'Pomp and Circumstance' march in mind, which Benson described in his diary as 'wizard-like'. Two years later he became a Fellow of Magdalene, having been appointed joint editor of the letters of Queen Victoria. In 1915 he became President of Magdalene (Senior Fellow) and three years later, Master (the boss), a post he held until his death.

Elgar's music, even more than Benson's words, ensured the place in the nation's heart that 'Land of Hope and Glory' continues to occupy. The 'Pomp and Circumstance' marches drew their title from Act III, Scene iii of Shakespeare's *Othello*, extolling the glory (the pomp) and the conduct (the circumstance) of war. The first two were composed in 1901, when the world had what we would now consider a naïve, over-romantic view of war. As the First World War loomed, an extra verse was added to encourage the troops as they set forth for France. By October 1919, however, Elgar had written his haunting 'Cello Concerto', in which his changed attitude to warfare is plain to hear. It is therefore rather ironic that he is probably most famous for an early piece expressing an attitude to war and empire that even he abrogated later in life.

Nevertheless, the popularity, widespread use and national associations of this basically secular piece cannot be ignored. The tune is so striking and rich that the passion, commitment and sheer enjoyment of singing it engenders ranks it with the best hymn tunes. And it can be used as such, to the words of 'At the name of Jesus'. If you have never come across this pairing before, perhaps try it (the last two lines need to be repeated):

At the name of Jesus
Every knee shall bow,
Every tongue confess him
King of glory now:
'Tis the Father's pleasure
We should call him Lord,
Who from the beginning
Was the mighty Word.

(WORDS FROM PHILIPPIANS 2:9–11: CAROLINE NOEL, 1817–77)

What do you think? Singing these words to that tune needs to be done

… the purpose of nationhood is to give coherence to diversity, not to promote enmity

cautiously. Yet the idea of praising God, in his own words, by using a tune that was originally about the glory of war and nation, and transforming it into a hymn of praise to the glorious King of all nations, seems to be a way of reminding ourselves of the vanities of human nationalism and perhaps even rescues the music for a greater cause. ∎

Reading for reflection

Philippians 2:1–11

Music to listen to

'Pomp and Circumstance' March No.1, from Opus 39. The choral version is the *Coronation Ode*, Op. 44, No. 7, 'Land of Hope and Glory', and is available in that version, recorded by the English Northern Philharmonia and Leeds Festival Chorus, conducted by Paul Daniel on Naxos 8.553981.

Four
to follow

David Winter is a well-known writer and broadcaster, who is retired from parish ministry. He contributes to 'New Daylight' Bible reading notes and has most recently written 'Pilgrim's Way' for BRF. A former Head of Religious Broadcasting at the BBC, he has both Celtic and Anglo-Saxon blood in his veins.

Andrew for Scotland, George for England, Patrick for Ireland and David for Wales: the lives of the patron saints of the British Isles span about 600 years of Christian history. Andrew was, of course, one of the apostles of Jesus. George, the details of his life obscured by subsequent legend and pious fiction, probably lived in the third century. Patrick can be fairly reliably placed in the fifth century and David equally reliably in the sixth. The last two were born somewhere in the west of Britain—David very probably on the western coast of Wales.

Historical details are probably less important in the creation of a suitable patron saint than the person's accepted character, strengths and example. On that basis, the patron saints of the British Isles seem to exemplify many of the aspirations of the nations that honour them. They certainly offer between them a rewarding picture of discipleship, courage and commitment, as well as a deep and inspiring spirituality.

The apostle Andrew

Andrew's role as one of Christ's apostles is somewhat overshadowed by that of his outspoken and headstrong brother, Simon Peter. Peter became the undisputed leader of the Twelve and, despite his impulsive and sometimes unnerving swings of character, a major figure in the emerging Church after the Ascension. We tend to overlook the fact that it was his brother Andrew who brought Peter to Christ. Having himself 'found' the one he recognised as the Messiah, Andrew immediately went and sought out his brother. 'He brought Simon to Jesus', John tells us (1:42, NRSV)—surely one of the most important pieces of personal evangelism in the history of Christianity!

Later, by the Sea of Galilee, they were both called to follow Jesus, which they did without hesitation. Andrew, while not enjoying the high profile of his brother, was, with him, one of the first two disciples to be called to follow Jesus, and he usually follows Peter, James and John in the Gospel lists of the apostles. Tradition, some of it very early, suggests that he preached the gospel in Greece and was martyred by crucifixion in about 60AD. Certainly his cross—the saltire (in the form of the letter X)—was associated with him from medieval times onwards, and is now, of course, the St Andrew's Cross of Scotland. It is said that he refused to be crucified on a similar cross to Jesus, feeling unworthy of the comparison.

What we know of Andrew suggests a man of simple, committed faith, who longed to share what he had found with others and did so in an unassuming yet courageous way. It is surely not too fanciful to see some of those characteristics in, for instance, the great missionary figures of

⌐ … a rewarding picture of discipleship, courage and commitment

> … that it was **his brother Andrew who brought Peter to Christ**

Scotland like David Livingstone and Mary Slessor.

George the soldier

George is rather different. If we take the most reliable of the traditions about him, he was a soldier, presumably in the Roman army, who became a Christian and was martyred during the persecutions of Diocletian and Maximian in about 303AD. Not surprisingly, he was taken up by the Crusaders as their patron, which is probably how he became associated with England, although there is no suggestion from the little we know about his life that he would have approved of taking up arms to defend the rights of Christians over against other people.

The story of George and the dragon is, sadly, almost certainly fiction. We are told that the country was being terrorised by a dragon and, to appease it, the king's daughter was chosen by lot as a sacrifice. George rode to her rescue, took her girdle to bind the dragon and led it to the people, saying that he would slay it if they all believed in Jesus Christ and were baptised. Not surprisingly, they

... a courageous refusal to deny the faith in the face of opposition

... a simple and sincere spirituality and deep pastoral care

agreed. Largely because it was included in a book called *Golden Legends*, the story was enormously popular in the Middle Ages, not only in England but across Europe.

Nevertheless, we can see in George some of the characteristics of the English people, certainly in the field of military courage but also perhaps in a courageous refusal to deny the faith in the face of opposition. The dedicated 'Christian soldier' is a metaphor much loved of Victorian hymn writers, but it is one we can also find in the letters of Paul. There *is* an element of conflict and

warfare involved in the Christian life, and in honouring George we are recognising that faith requires faithfulness, even, as the book of Revelation says, 'until death' (2:10).

Patrick, man of faith

Patrick offers us a picture of a simple, straightforward man, one who always lamented his lack of 'learning', who by faith became an outstanding disciple of Jesus, a leader in the Church and an inspiration to countless people across Ireland and Britain. Although brought up in a Christian home in Britain, he described himself as 'not knowing the true God' until he was taken captive by Irish pirates and held as a slave in that country for six years. He used the time to pray, and during those dark years he came to a firm belief in the faith of his father (a deacon) and his grandfather (a priest).

Escaping from captivity, he made his way by sea back to Britain, received some theological training and was ordained priest. He eventually returned to Ireland, where he was made bishop of the Irish in succession to Palladius. He established his see at Armagh, from which base he set out on missionary journeys across the northern half of Ireland, as well as western Britain.

His writings are the first authentic literature of the British Church. They speak of a simple and sincere spirituality and deep pastoral care, which it would be fair to describe as characteristics of Irish Christianity at its best.

David, the eloquent evangelist

David, like Patrick, was a child of the Celtic Church, which contributed so profoundly to the shaping of the faith in the British Isles in the so-called 'Dark Ages' and the early medieval period. He was probably born and educated at Hen Vynyw on the west coast of Wales before being ordained and establishing a peripatetic ministry across Pembrokeshire and then the whole of south Wales. At some point he was made a bishop, as there is a record of him visiting Ireland, where people received communion from 'Bishop David of Wales'. He founded a monastery at Menevia (later known as St David's). There he acquired the nickname 'Aquaticus' because he and his monks drank only water and ate only vegetables and bread.

He was evidently a powerful preacher, who was invited to address a synod called to deal with the problem of the Pelagian heresy. Pelagius was a British-born theologian in the early fifth century who argued that the first steps to salvation could be taken before the gift of grace, a view sternly dismissed by Augustine,

> ... a **powerful preacher**

among others. David spoke with such power that, it is said, the assembled company insisted he should be made archbishop of Wales. The site of this synod is now known as Llandewi Brefi (the town of David on the little hill).

We can perhaps see in David the inspiration of generations of eloquent and powerful Welsh orators and preachers, from David Lloyd George to Martyn Lloyd Jones. Even today preaching is probably held in higher respect in Wales than anywhere else in Britain. But David was more than a great preacher—he was, like many in the Celtic Church, a passionate evangelist and a deeply devout and rigorously disciplined Christian.

With four patron saints like these, the people of Britain can never claim that they have no role models for the life of faith. Apostolic witness, Christian soldier, humble disciple, eloquent preacher of the gospel— what more could we ask? ∎

The beautiful game

Kevin Scully is the rector of St Matthew's, Bethnal Green, in London's East End. He has written 'Into Your Hands' and 'Five Impossible Things to Believe Before Christmas' for BRF. He is a season ticket holder at Leyton Orient.

There is a bloke in a pub I know who is a passionate Manchester United fan. Come to think of it, that is putting it mildly. He is more a fanatic, an obsessive, who, to be honest, cannot seem to speak of anything else but his beloved team. You can see his eyes fade to detachment from those around him when the subject changes from football. Even the weather, except in relation to how it impacts on the past, current or forthcoming games involving Man U (about which he is, like other matters pertaining to the heroes of Old Trafford, encyclopedic in his coverage) cannot draw him out of his shell.

It is somewhat easy to dismiss this man. After all, no one I know (even me!) would be as tedious as that. That depends on who you talk to. I support a lower level league team, Leyton Orient, and I have for some years been a season ticket holder. A few years ago, through a combination of bad weather and a good run in the FA Cup preliminaries causing the postponement of scheduled fixtures, the Mighty Os had a succession of home games within a concentrated few weeks. Tuesday nights and Saturday afternoons would find me in my seat in the East Stand.

One night, out of sheer desperation to be in my company, my wife said she would come to a game. I was delighted to have her with me for what I see as a harmless recreation. It was a cold, wet, miserable evening both on and off the pitch. As she shivered next to me, watching nothing much happening on the field, she exploded, 'For heaven's sake, why don't they just get the ball, run to the other end of the field and kick it in?'

I congratulated her on mastering the basics of the game. She will relate the incident to anyone who will listen and go on to tell them how boring football is. She swears that nothing—not even an FA Cup final game at Wembley—will entice her to go to a game of football again. I try to argue with her conclusions, concede that what she saw that night was far from scintillating, and attempt to tell her that not all games are like that. Yet my wife, like the bloke in the pub, has made a decision.

Some self-examination might be useful here. For all my arguments, I am probably as guilty as the pub bore in using football—or at least, my support of a team—as part of my identity. I am a person, in a place, with relationships, who supports a League One team.

There are three other kinds of football nuts. There is the supporter who turns out only for big events (up to 4000 Leyton Orient fans— more than the then-average crowd for a home game— turned out for a fourth-round FA Cup clash with a Premiership side). Then there

© Photos.com

are the 'experts' who watch the matches between nations. As the fixtures head toward games of more significance, their knowledge increases and their viewing time becomes more protected. Yet after the event they seem to fade into the woodwork. More interesting than these are the people who just love the game. They look at any game, from little league to international ties, with a loving eye. Football gives them a purpose beyond the sectional or sectarian. They have a passion, but it is both quiet and focused.

It has to be admitted that the Christian faith and how it is practised could replace much of what I have said about football. The range from boringly obsessive to quietly supportive of local endeavours, to people who turn out for big events, is more or less the same. It is

He is more than a fanatic, who... **cannot seem to speak of anything else but his beloved team**

What they believe... reflects something deep in them

People who, despite all the fuss, glamour and agitation, are confident in who they are

often a debate among church leaders and regular members how far these people should be accommodated. Are the attenders who never miss a Christmas midnight mass really, as they often claim for themselves, regulars?

Their opinions matter—be it over the Bible, music, ritual or architecture—and will be expressed with the fervour of the person who never misses a service and who, for whatever reason, believes that a piece of furniture in one particular place is theirs. Saying that runs the risk of belittling them. What they believe reflects something deep in them. They associate with Jesus and they believe they are entitled to full recognition. It is, quite simply, part of their identity.

Nothing causes quite so many arguments in church circles as how certain things might be defined. The whole history of denominations denying other branches of the faith a place in heaven is evidence enough. A race through history will find plenty of fodder for argument: disputes over creeds, or even clauses within a creed, the irreparable break over one part of doctrine or practice or the nature or

gender of priests. These disputes are not limited to cross-border skirmishes. The fractious words and actions of competing parts of Anglicanism, even those who have appointed themselves the saviours of the Communion, in the past few years show that there is plenty to argue about within a group.

Much of the controversy stems from what we believe to be the basis of our identity. Many people held out hope that a common identity, even if only a limited one, would be achieved by a number of churches agreeing to a recognition of each other's baptism. Those involved in what is known as the 1982 Lima Declaration had hoped that this would be a basis on which to start bridging the gaps between them. It did not, and probably cannot, fully succeed. There is just too much at stake.

Maybe something like the third kind of football fans is needed in Christianity. People who, despite all the fuss, glamour and agitation, are confident in who they are, knowing they can answer that question Jesus put to Peter, 'Who do you say that I am?' (Matthew 16:15, NIV). ∎

Composed Upon Westminster Bridge September 3, 1802

Earth has not anything to show more fair:
Dull would he be of soul who could pass by
A sight so touching in its majesty:
This City now doth, like a garment, wear
The beauty of the morning; silent, bare,
Ships, towers, domes, theatres, and temples lie
Open unto the fields, and to the sky;
All bright and glittering in the smokeless air.
Never did the sun more beautifully steep
In his first splendour, valley, rock, or hill;
Ne'er saw I, never felt, a calm so deep!
The river glideth at his own sweet will:
Dear God! the very houses seem asleep;
And all that mighty heart is lying still!

WILLIAM WORDSWORTH (1770–1850)

Teaching people
to 'fish'

Kelli Ross is Director of Communications for Five Talents International, where she oversees all aspects of marketing and communications, including direct mail, website, social networking and graphic design.

Thanks to the income from her small food business, Ahok, who is a single mother living in Lietnhom, Sudan, is now able to send all five of her children to school. Akot, her ten-year-old son, has begun first grade—one step toward his dream of becoming a doctor.

'I love my mother,' Akot says. 'She gives me milk and biscuits every day. I also love my school uniform; I look smart in school.'

Ahok started her business with a US$75 loan. She has now received a second loan of $150 from the village bank in Lietnhom, which was established by a consortium of organisations, including Five Talents, World Concern and the Episcopal Church of Sudan.

Five Talents was created as a long-term response to the ravages of poverty that debilitate communities in developing countries. It was established by a resolution passed at the 1998 Lambeth Conference, where the founders, including Anglican church leaders, talked about the plight of the poor and those dying of famine, HIV/AIDS and other diseases. They wanted not only to assist but also to guard the dignity of the poor, many of whom survive on $1 a day, by supporting them in small businesses.

Based on the parable of the talents (Matthew

Ahok is the mother of five boys, owner of two small businesses, and has recently been named chairlady of the Amot Wuot Community Bank in Lietnohm, Sudan

A long-term response to the ravages of poverty

25:14–30), Five Talents strives to live out and encourage others to know of and use their God-given abilities and talents. 'Rather than try to combat poverty from the top down, microenterprise fights poverty from the ground up by working directly to change the lives of those most affected by poverty,' said Bishop Simon Chiwanga of Tanzania and Five Talents co-founder during a celebration event at the most recent Lambeth Conference.

Today, Five Talents works in Bolivia, the Dominican Republic, India, Indonesia, Kenya, the Philippines, Peru, Tanzania, Uganda, as well as Sudan. In 2008, it had an impact on the lives of 20,000 people—each $200 loan affects up to six people.

Five Talents targets those at the bottom of the economic ladder through a grassroots network within the worldwide Anglican Communion. It identifies and supports indigenous partner organisations

Microenterprise fights poverty from the ground up by working directly to change the lives of those most affected by poverty

... places that are smaller, riskier, poorer than most

Akot is a 10-year old living in Lietnohm, Sudan, who now attends school thanks to the income from his mother's small businesses

working in microenterprise development, which serve their communities with integrity and transparency. The Anglican Church has a very strong presence in Africa (approximately 50 million members), and the network covers all of Asia and Latin America. This provides a powerful means to administer the microloans and give training and support.

'Microfinance is now centre stage of the development agenda. The 2006 Nobel Peace Prize was awarded to a Bangladeshi microfinance bank and its founder—the Peace Prize, not the Economics Prize. This testifies to the broad impact that microfinance has on communities and livelihoods, helping the poor while preserving their dignity,' Rowan Williams, Archbishop of Canterbury and International Patron of Five Talents, said recently.

'Microfinance works. It is aligned with personal interests and responsibilities, while the group method brings accountability, and the savings component encourages planning. It is also an extremely cost effective means of contributing to the Millennium Development Goals. The Church has a distinct advantage in delivering microfinance services, through its local presence, credibility and network. I am pleased that Five Talents joins those who are taking forward this vital work in the worldwide Communion.'

Where grant programmes have failed, Five Talents has provided platforms for long-term growth and stability. By teaching basic business skills before providing loan capital, Five Talents ensures that the entrepreneurs and communities benefit now and in the future. It is a very practical and sound approach to fighting poverty. Five Talents President and CEO, Craig Cole, explains how it is not a handout programme: 'We are teaching the poor that they have value and the power to transform their lives and the lives of their families.'

As a viable tool to help the poor, microcredit is one of the few charitable models that keeps donations in circulation. As loans are repaid with interest (repayment ranges from 85 to 100 percent), that money is lent out again, on average twice each year for years to come. And it is in places like southern Sudan where Five Talents works—places that are smaller, riskier, poorer than most.

Despite the hardships of the past few months, the programme that helped Ahok has already replicated itself with the start of two new village and savings loan associations in the nearby town of Luanyeker. Each has 20 women. Ahok challenges other women to start businesses so they too can provide for their families, and she has set an example worth following: single-handedly, she has sent her oldest son to secondary school in Uganda as there are no high schools in Lietnhom.

'I do not know what would have happened to my family and children if Five Talents had not come to our town,' Ahok said. 'Before they came, I was not able to buy enough food, school books or uniforms for my children. Now, I am able to support my children with all they need.'

Person by person, loan by loan, Five Talents helps liberate the God-given talents of poor individuals and families and give them a chance to make something better of their lives. And it's the children of these microentrepreneurs who will feel the difference for a lifetime. By providing parents with small loans, Five Talents is able to provide their children with healthy meals and a safe living environment.

Before Five Talents helped, six-year-old Rosita and her family suffered from severe malnutrition. She and her family had moved to Lima from a small Peruvian city in the Amazon jungle. Her parents searched in

Thanks to God, we have improved our business, we do not beg for food any more, and my mother can now buy food to cook in our house vain for odd jobs, just to survive in the capital. Rosita's mother, Maria, tells of how they went to bed many nights with empty stomachs: 'We would get meals at a community food kitchen but suffered from food poisoning several times.' This forced Rosita's parents to risk sickness or choose hunger for their family.

When Rosita's stepfather, Roberto, received his first loan of $170, he invested the money in the family's handicraft business, making necklaces, bracelets and earrings out of beads made of seeds from the Amazon. The business is generating a monthly income of $195, and with this money, they have purchased two machines in order to meet increased demand for their Amazon bead jewellery. 'Thanks to God, we have improved our business, we do not beg for food any more, and my mother can now buy food to cook in our house,' Rosita says.

Malnutrition isn't the only battle parents are fighting. Based on enrolment data, about 72 million children of primary school age in the developing world were not in school in 2005; 57 percent of them were girls, according to the Millennium Development Goals Report 2007. With income from a small business, however, mothers and fathers are able to pay school fees for their children.

Irene is able to attend 4th grade because her mother, Jane, was able to access a small loan in order to start a small business. Jane now has the money to pay for Irene's school fees

Irene is one of the top students in her fourth-grade class, and her mother, Jane, is very proud of her achievements. Without the help of Jane's loan group in Thika, Kenya, Irene may not have been able to attend—or have had such success—in school. Since 2004, Jane has invested her small loans in her vegetable garden and rabbit business, using the profits to pay for her children's school fees and buy them clothing and nutritious food.

'I also really hope that with the next loan my mum gets, she will build us a nice home,' Irene says. The family is currently living in a two-room house with iron sheets for a roof and mud walls. Irene dreams of one day becoming an environmental scientist, so that she can teach others what she knows about trees, animals, flowers and food crops.

There is the saying, 'Give a person a fish and you feed them for a day, but teach a person to fish and you feed them for a lifetime.' At Five Talents, our hope is to transform the lives of those we touch. We want to 'teach people to fish and, at the same time, help them discover a pride and an identity as fishermen, resulting in feeding them, their family and their community for life'. We are seeing this transformation in men, women and children around the world, like five-year-old Esther.

Since Esther's mother, Phiong, joined a loan group in Jakarta, Indonesia, and expanded her cake business, she can now afford to buy nutritious food and to pay for Esther's school fees—she's in kindergarten this year! Phiong owed a loan shark $820. Without the means to pay it back, she became desperate and contemplated committing suicide.

That's when members of the Anggrek Ciracas loan group stepped in to help. They encouraged her and prayed for her, asking God to strengthen her and to help her overcome her family's problems and improve their finances. Phiong received a $43 loan to purchase the supplies she needed to continue operating her small business, selling traditional cakes at a school in East Jakarta. 'Now, I can drink milk and pay my school tuition fees,' Esther said. 'Mum said she will start selling noodles so that my brother and I can continue to go to school. I pray that the Lord Jesus continues to help us.' ■

Because of her mother's ability to take a loan and expand her cake business, Esther now has the opportunity to attend Kindergarten

Our hope is to transform the lives of those we touch

Five Talents' ongoing work is supported by a staff based in Virginia, USA, and an office in London. For more information, visit www.fivetalents.org.

Limbo

Brad Lincoln, along with his family, served with INF as missionary in Nepal from 2001, returning to live in the UK in 2006, where Brad now works as a company director. Brad's work is international in nature, so he spends plenty of time in airport departure lounges and in the air, where he often finds time to reflect on the lessons that come with switching to very different cultures.

I cry only at films I see on aircrafts, sitting alone, sometimes in Business Class, allowing a few tears to gather at the corners of my eyes, brushing them away before they reach my cheeks. At home this seldom happens. My *terra firma* tears are reserved for moments of frustration when I just can't hold in the repressed feelings of dislocation. Then they burst from me and course unchecked. When they cease I am free to resume the armour of apparent stability and security that Western society seems to demand of me and everyone else I know. Especially at church.

In no-man's land I seem more able to acknowledge my feelings, more able to be honest with myself, freer to allow my emotions to run with the films. Perhaps when airborne, in neither one country nor the other, my physical situation briefly reflects my spiritual and emotional status and that is why I feel more at home in the air than on the ground.

It wasn't always that way. There was a time when I knew exactly where I was from, where I belonged. I was a confident, educated man, secure in the illusion that my talents and abilities would be enough to get by. I had a good job, a great CV, an easily serviced mortgage, time and money to enjoy holidays and give generously to my church, and the energy to engage in supporting others.

Of course, as a Christian I professed a belief that attributed all my blessings to God and agreed with the doctrine that emphasised my reliance on God. The reality was, however, that I treated

© Photos.com

his care and provision more as a spiritual insurance policy than something as ever-present and life-sustaining as air. If I felt a spiritual twinge I could pop to the local 'surgery' for a five-minute consultation and a prescriptive dose of scriptural advice. More often than not, I didn't even need to speak to anyone and could just get a repeat prescription myself. Once, even, I crashed and had to visit the A&E department followed by an extended period of rehabilitation. In those moments I was especially grateful that I had kept up my church attendance and my sporadic attempts at genuine daily communion through speed-read Bible notes, like some form of holy National Insurance contribution to ensure that the vital services were there for me when I really needed them.

But then, my family and I were called out into the unknown, to work in Nepal, and I went gladly. Despite the best efforts of our sending agency to prepare us, we went without fully understanding the sense of identity we were sacrificing. If I'm honest, if I'd known the cost, I'm not absolutely certain I would have been so obedient. Serving in Nepal, we found a life where the spiritual was an ever-present phenomenon.

We were baptised into that life as we lived for the first four months in community, sharing every meal and trial and adjustment with other new missionaries. In sharing we deepened relationships a little and learned a daily routine in which prayer covered every meeting, each day of language learning, each meal. The world in which we then became immersed, living on an urban street among Hindu and Muslim neighbours, was vibrant with the spiritual. During the festivals we were bombarded with reminders of the local belief systems. Any tree or rock might represent one of the gods, the temples we passed each day were a sensory assault of

We know it lacks something **we find hard to express without the language of heaven**

... when my whole being takes flight

smells and colours, and at night during *dosaii* (the biggest of the Hindu festivals, lasting ten days) prayers and music blared constantly. To pray was not an option but a requirement if one was to prevail against the overwhelming spiritual bombardment. It was at that time that I learnt to start each day sitting on my roof, welcoming the morning sun and, with it, acknowledging the daily life-sustaining force of God.

Our return to the UK, after five years, was an event we anticipated as something of a relief from the constant engagement, like troops returning from the front line. Our guard slipped. In the UK we encountered a more insidious cold war of subterfuge, where the attacks were more subtle. The forces ranged against us were indifference and complacency. To misquote Kevin Spacey's character in *The Usual Suspects*, 'The greatest trick the devil pulled was to convince the world that he didn't exist.' As fish out of water, unused to dealing with the dryness, we looked to those who had supported us so ably when we had been overseas, and found that their attention was elsewhere. They could not comprehend our dislocation from what should have been a familiar society.

Believers and atheists alike feel a deep urge to reach out for something more permanent, more enduring, and closer to perfection. All the while we are rooted to this earthly life, we know it lacks something that we find hard to express without the language of heaven. We would break free if we could and fly if we knew how. Those of us who have made our departure plans, bought our tickets and have passed through security into customs now sit in departures, impatiently eyeing the screens for signs that it will soon be time to travel.

Our return from service overseas was a journey to find that 'home' is a misnomer. We've tasted a life in which our lives obeyed a spiritual rhythm that we have failed to rediscover in the UK, and the fact that we do not fully belong to this world has been made clear.

But we know that a return to Nepal is not the answer, because we yearn not for warfare but for a time of spiritual harmony. It would be wrong to characterise us as 'returning missionaries' and to diagnose our sense of dissatisfaction as a difficulty in readjusting. In learning to live spiritual lives, one small part of us has left, I hope never to return. I am just anxiously waiting for the time when my whole being takes flight and I am called to my true home. ∎

Adventuring in
prayer

Adrian Chatfield is a Trinidadian priest and has spent the past 20 years in theological education in England and South Africa, exercising his ministry in tandem with his teaching. When he's not teaching worship, spirituality or Anglicanism, he loves preaching, leading retreats, cycling and playing Scrabble® with his wife Jill.

There is a playful side of me that enjoys hearing people ask why Ridley Hall has set up a Centre for Prayer and the Spiritual Life, more than a century after its foundation as a theological college. After all, hasn't it always been a centre for spiritual formation? The Simeon Centre can't be a retreat house, and it's certainly not a new monastic foundation, as anyone who spends time in a modern theological college will attest!

The truthful, somewhat mischievous answer is that it is one of God's surprises, something new that God has called us to in a dry season, when many in the churches are tempted away from prayer by busyness. The story of its conception and birth is certainly improbable. A number of years ago our chaplain, Jane Keiller, read about a centre for prayer and spiritual direction training in the USA. A dream began to emerge for something similar here, and

> The dream **caught the imagination**

… begin to turn them into a reality

A gift of resourcing, renewing and refreshing the church's life of prayer

after a sabbatical visit to a number of such places, the idea was mooted for a centre in East Anglia with Cambridge as the obvious base, given Jane's roles in the Hall and Diocese of Ely.

The dream caught the imagination of a number of people. At one point it looked as if it might become a diocesan venture but funding seemed an insuperable problem. Plans were subsequently drawn up for what such a centre might look like at Ridley, if only the funds were available. Then, extraordinarily, just before the plans were due to be presented to the College Council, a benefactor asked the then principal, Chris Cocksworth, if there was a chance that the Hall might need funds for some project in the area of prayer. And so, in October 2007, the Centre was born, named after the Simeon who, having recognised in Jesus the Saviour of the world, knew that he could 'depart in peace', and also after Charles Simeon, Rector of Holy Trinity Cambridge for 52 years from 1783, a man of deep prayer and gospel discipline.

Dream into reality

It was a surprise and a delight to be asked to take Jane's dream and the Hall's plans, and begin to turn them into a reality as the centre's first director. It continues to be a privilege to work alongside her and learn from her. In essence, the task is very simple. So far as the Ridley Hall community is concerned, the Centre is testimony to the fact that our spiritual formation is a prerequisite for sharing in God's mission. All our praying, all our worship, all our training in the spiritual disciplines are the Centre's brief, to which the whole community contributes. We are also committed to the academic and practical teaching of prayer and spirituality in the Hall and in the Cambridge Theological Federation (the cluster of institutions training people for public ministry in the churches), and to ensuring a high profile for the spiritual formation of those whom we train.

The most exciting and innovative part of the Centre's work, however, is what I like to think of as the Hall's gift to the wider church—a gift of resourcing, renewing and refreshing the church's life of prayer. This is beginning to happen in two settings: at Ridley itself and around the country, because we are not tied to a building. In Ridley, this includes termly quiet days that are open to the wider community, conferences and a sabbatical programme. At the time of writing, plans were well in hand for a residential conference in September this year, on *Restoring Prayer*, with the keynote speaker being the American pastor and writer, Eugene Peterson. Other speakers included Anne Dyer, Alister McGrath and Paula Gooder, and we planned a range of practical workshops on ways and contexts of praying.

The Centre's vision also includes the training of spiritual directors, as there is a burgeoning hunger for spiritual direction among Christians of all traditions. Both Jane and I offer spiritual direction ourselves but the demand is greater than the supply. So the Simeon Centre is committed to working within diocesan structures as well as the ecumenical Cambridge Course in Spirituality and the Art of Spiritual Direction to provide such training, believing that it is more important to build relationships and develop networks than to try to do everything ourselves. Further afield, we welcome invitations to work with churches or groups of churches on developing resources of this kind, through leading parish weekends on prayer, helping to plan regional programmes and speaking at conferences.

Long before I came to the Centre, I had a

In a world where believing seems impossible for many… the proportion of people who pray remains high

Faithful to God not only in what we do for him but also in who we are towards him

nagging but unformed sense of how important prayer is as a means of evangelism. In a world where believing seems impossible for many and belonging to any institution is unfashionable and risky, the proportion of people who pray remains high. My own sister, who wouldn't pretend to be a Christian, regularly asks me to pray for her business, which I am glad to do. But when I was applying to work at the Centre, I asked her whether she would pray for me and, somewhat to my surprise, she agreed. We haven't had a conversation about it since, and I'm not quite sure what she thought she was doing, but it felt much easier than 'evangelising' her. It's certainly been the main way in which we talk, however superficially, about the things of God. So discovering that one of the aims of the Centre is to foster 'prayer as evangelism' has been personally very significant. We hope that at some time in the future, we will be able to gather others who have a similar passion and belief together, to see how we may better use this gift from God to win people for Christ.

A new community?

Of all the things that have surprised me about this venture, the Simeon Community is the most surprising, and I'm still not quite sure how it came about. Increasingly, it feels like the most important aspect of what we are doing, though the shape and direction still eludes us. Early on in the Centre's life, we felt that God was saying to us that he wanted us to form a dispersed intentional community, which would be committed to praying for the Centre on a regular basis, but also exploring from a Christian perspective the cliché that the world is desperately hungry to experience significant community. It has been a real encouragement that a number of those who have joined have been drawn to us by a deep sense of a call from God, without necessarily understanding why. We'd love to have more friends like that, willing to risk setting out on an unpredictable journey with us in Christ. As we explore what the Simeon Community means, we are in conversation with a range of 'fresh expressions' of prayer community, including the Boiler Rooms that have come out of the 24–7 movement, discovering what we have in common and what we may learn from them.

Some of this is still inevitably vague: we long to do so many things, but at the heart of it all is our call to be a prayer- and worship-shaped people, faithful to God not only in what we do for him but also, and primarily, in who we are towards him and with

A number of those who have joined have been drawn to us **by a deep sense of a call from God**

him. There is an open invitation to come to events that we put on, and we particularly hope that the *Restoring Prayer* conference will have encouraged many who long to grow in their prayerful relationship with God. But our greatest desire is to hold hands with others who are seeking to resource the church, to build networks, and to 'equip the saints for the work of ministry, for building up the body of Christ' (Ephesians 4:12, NRSV). ∎

To find out more about the Centre, please email Rosemary Kew at rak44@cam.ac.uk, ring Adrian on 01223 741090 or go to our website www.ridley.cam.ac.uk/scabout.html.

Nation

Simon Keyes is the Director of St Ethelburga's Centre for Reconciliation and Peace. The Centre arose from the ruins of the tiny medieval church in the City of London, which was destroyed by an IRA bomb in 1993.

Sunday

'Let all the nations be gathered together...'

ISAIAH 43:9 (KJV).

Awareness and praise are the keystones of my prayer life, but so often I am shaken off balance by stories of brutality from around the world. I reach for a prayer which we wrote at St Ethelburga's on 7 July 2005, the day of the London bombings.

A prayer for an end to violence

God of Life

Every act of violence
Between myself and another
    Destroys a part of your creation

Stir in my heart
A renewed sense of reverence
    For all life

Give me vision to recognise your spirit
In every human being
    However they behave towards me

Make possible the impossible
By cultivating in me
    The fertile seed of healing love

May I play my part
In breaking the cycle of violence
By realising that
    Peace begins with me

I will spend this week roaming the open spaces of this prayer.

Monday

God of Life

I breathe, I think, I feel, I love, I create, I sin. I share this unfathomable dimension of consciousness with billions of other beings, perhaps even in billions of universes. I cannot begin to conceive what creation means, but I know that I AM.

Alleluia!

Tuesday

Every act of violence
Between myself and another
*   Destroys a part of your creation*

I watch the news and realise that we have forgotten how to disagree. Televised protagonists of conflicts worldwide seem to solicit my approval of, or at least my acquiescence in, their violence. I must resist, but what have my own actions, words and thoughts destroyed today?

Alleluia!

Wednesday

Stir in my heart
A renewed sense of reverence
*   For all life.*

I watch a flock of starlings diving and wheeling, thousands of bodies forming a huge curtain dancing in the wind. How do I tune into that vast harmonic that binds me to all the human family and to life in all its myriad forms? Will any of the thoughts, schemes, beliefs that separate us cast the slightest shadow in the light of I AM?

Alleluia!

Thursday

Give me vision to recognise your spirit
In every human being
*   However they behave towards me*

In sweltering heat, I camped beside Lake Galilee and wandered the hills where Jesus spoke. Blessed are those who suffer persecution. Can I accept that my enemy may be my best teacher?

Alleluia!

Friday

Make possible the impossible
By cultivating in me
  The fertile seed of healing love

It's below zero and snowing, yet there's a new flower on the jasmine in St Ethelburga's garden. What does it mean to prepare and tend that moist, dark soil in which the silent miracle of germination can occur?

Alleluia!

Saturday

May I play my part
In breaking the cycle of violence
By realising that
  Peace begins with me

My daily responsibility to take the risks of love will never cease. The water looks dangerous but if I were to throw myself into God's deep floods, how far would the ripple go?

Alleluia!

Musings of a middle-aged mystic

Veronica Zundel is a journalist, author and contributor to 'New Daylight'. She has also written 'The Time of our Lives' (2007) and 'Crying for the Light' (2008) for BRF. She lives in north London.

As the daughter of refugees from the Nazis, with close family destroyed in the Holocaust, I am probably the last person who should be writing on the theme of 'nation'! To misquote Goering on culture, 'When I hear the word "nation" I reach for my gun'—or I would, if I weren't a pacifist... Unbridled nationalism has been one of the curses of the last century, and not just 70 years ago but in recent memory.

In the Bible, too, 'the nations' is often a negative term, referring to the cultures around the Israelites who served pagan gods. For instance, in Psalm 2, the psalmist asks, 'Why do the nations conspire, and the peoples plot in vain... against the Lord and his anointed?' (vv. 1–2, NRSV). Job points out that the fate of nations is not self-determined but in the hand of God: 'He makes nations great, then destroys them; he enlarges nations, then leads them away' (12:23). And Isaiah says that in God's perspective, 'Even the nations are like a drop from a bucket, and are accounted as dust on the scales' (40:15).

Yet in the New Testament, Peter writes to the believers that they are 'a chosen race, a royal priesthood, a holy nation, God's own people' (1 Peter 2:9). In Christ our citizenship

The idea of a nation can teach us about community and solidarity

God's desire is to **transform all** aspects of our human cultures

is based on God's kingdom, not on what passport we hold.

Personally, I have never felt truly a member of any political entity called a 'nation'—except perhaps for a few moments during the Last Night of the Proms when I hear 'Rule Britannia' sung! I'm not quite English, having been raised in a European-cultured household, yet I'm not Austrian either, never having lived there. So the concept of my being, as a Christian, a 'resident alien' is one that has a strong personal meaning for me.

But can the concept of 'nation' as a geographical identity be redeemed? My mind goes to Acts 17, where Paul, preaching to the philosophically-minded Athenians, declares: 'From one ancestor [God] made all nations to inhabit the whole earth, and he allotted the times of their existence

and the boundaries of the places where they would live, so that they would search for God and perhaps grope for him and find him' (vv. 26–27).

This seems to suggest that human cultures, including our tendency to set up national units and boundaries, are not just a product of a fallen, divided world. They are a way in which we may encounter God and discover aspects of what it means to follow God. Nations develop particular characters, which can be used for God's purposes, and the idea of a nation can teach us about community and solidarity.

I notice also, though, that Paul is careful to state that God made the nations 'from one ancestor'. Here is a biblical affirmation that there is really only one race, the human race, to which we all belong by birth.

I couldn't end this brief biblical survey without turning to Revelation 22, and its vision of the new Jerusalem: 'On either side of the river is the tree of life… and the leaves of the tree are for the healing of the nations' (v. 2). God's desire is to transform all aspects of our human cultures, bringing them under the loving rule of Christ—so the idea of nationhood, too, has a place in the new heavens and new earth for which we wait. No longer will it be a pretext for hostility, land-grabbing and war; instead different human groups will live together, respecting each other's differences and learning from them. I can't wait. ■

Our next issue

Our next issue will have both a new editor and a new format. The editor is the Rev Heather Fenton, who ran 'Coleg y Groes' Retreat House in North Wales for nearly 25 years. The theme will be 'Yesterday', followed later in 2010 by 'Today' and 'Tomorrow'. In the first of these we explore 'Yesterday' from different perspectives, starting with the very beginnings of the universe. We also think about the psalmist as he considers his personal yesterday—his own formation in the womb. Then we look back at our own 'yesterdays' and finally explore the Eucharist as encompassing past, present and future—which will lead us easily into the themes for the next two issues.

Contact us at:

Quiet Spaces,
BRF,
15 The Chambers,
Vineyard, Abingdon
OX14 3FE
enquiries@brf.org.uk

QUIET SPACES SUBSCRIPTIONS

Quiet Spaces is published three times a year, in March, July and November. To take out a subscription, please complete this form, indicating the month in which you would like your subscription to begin.

❑ I would like to give a gift subscription (please complete both name and address sections below)

❑ I would like to take out a subscription myself (complete name and address details only once)

This completed coupon should be sent with appropriate payment to BRF. Alternatively, please write to us quoting your name, address, the subscription you would like for either yourself or a friend (with their name and address), the start date and credit card number, expiry date and signature if paying by credit card.

Gift subscription name _____

Gift subscription address _____

_____ Postcode _____

Please send beginning with the next March / July / November issue: *(delete as applicable)*

(please tick box)   UK   SURFACE   AIR MAIL

Quiet Spaces   ❑ £16.95   ❑ £18.45   ❑ £20.85

Please complete the payment details below and send your coupon, with appropriate payment to: BRF, 15 The Chambers, Vineyard, Abingdon OX14 3FE.

Name _____

Address _____

_____

Postcode _____ Telephone Number _____

Email _____

❑ Please do not email me any information about BRF publications

Method of payment: ❑ Cheque ❑ Mastercard ❑ Visa ❑ Maestro ❑ Postal Order

Card no. ⬜⬜⬜⬜ ⬜⬜⬜⬜ ⬜⬜⬜⬜ ⬜⬜⬜⬜ ⬜⬜⬜⬜

Valid from ⬜⬜ ⬜⬜   Expires ⬜⬜ ⬜⬜   Issue no. of Maestro card ⬜⬜⬜

Security Code ⬜⬜⬜

Signature _____ Date ___/___/___

All orders must be accompanied by the appropriate payment.
Please make cheques payable to BRF

❑ Please do not send me further information about BRF publications

PROMO REF: QSNATION

BRF is a Registered Charity